Little Brown Girl

AISHA SHAWQI

iUniverse books may be ordered through booksellers or by contacting:

iUniverse
1663 Liberty Drive
Bloomington, IN 47403
www.iuniverse.com
844-349-9409

Because of the dynamic nature of the Internet, any web addresses or links contained in this book may have changed since publication and may no longer be valid. The views expressed in this work are solely those of the author and do not necessarily reflect the views of the publisher, and the publisher hereby disclaims any responsibility for them.

Any people depicted in stock imagery provided by Getty Images are models, and such images are being used for illustrative purposes only.
Certain stock imagery © Getty Images.

ISBN: 978-1-6632-1208-5 (sc)
ISBN: 978-1-6632-0549-0 (hc)
ISBN: 978-1-6632-0548-3 (e)

Library of Congress Control Number: 2020925812

Print information available on the last page.

iUniverse rev. date: 12/30/2020

Little Brown Girl

Little brown girl as
pretty as can be.

Little brown girl as
tall as a tree.

Little brown girl so
small like a pea.

Little brown girl oh how
perfect you are to me.

Little brown girl you can be
anything you want to be.

Little brown girl you're
so amazing to me.

Little brown girl let your
light shine bright.

Little brown girl so
full of spice.

Little brown girl so
beautiful and nice.

Little brown girl with
such perfect skin.

Little brown girl you
don't have to fit in.

Little brown girl let your goals
stretch as far as the sea.

Little brown girl oh how
perfect you are to me.

Little brown girl you have
such big beautiful hair.

Printed in the United States
By Bookmasters